Nebraska
The Cornhusker State

Miriam Coleman

PowerKiDS press™

New York

Published in 2011 by The Rosen Publishing Group, Inc.
29 East 21st Street, New York, NY 10010

First Edition

Editor: Joanne Randolph
Book Design: Greg Tucker
Layout Design: Kate Laczynski
Photo Researcher: Jessica Gerweck

Photo Credits: Cover © SuperStock/age fotostock; p. 5 © www.istockphoto.com/MidwestWilderness; p. 7 © Jim Wark/age fotostock; p. 9 MPI/Stringer/Hulton Archive/Getty Images; pp. 11, 15, 17, 22 (tree, animal, bird, flower) Shutterstock.com; p. 13 Altrendo Nature/Getty Images; p. 19 Joel Sartore/Getty Images; p. 22 (Red Cloud) Buyenlarge/Getty Images; p. 22 (Gerald Ford) Dirck Halstead/Getty Images; p. 22 (Malcolm X) Michael Ochs Archives/Getty Images.

Library of Congress Cataloging-in-Publication Data

Coleman, Miriam.
   Nebraska : the Cornhusker State / Miriam Coleman. — 1st ed.
      p. cm. — (Our amazing states)
   Includes index.
   ISBN 978-1-4488-0656-0 (library binding) — ISBN 978-1-4488-0744-4 (pbk.) — ISBN 978-1-4488-0745-1 (6-pack)
   1. Nebraska—Juvenile literature. I. Title.
   F666.3.C65 2011
   978.2—dc22
                                              2009052016

Manufactured in the United States of America

CPSIA Compliance Information: Batch #WS10PK: For Further Information contact Rosen Publishing, New York, New York at 1-800-237-9932

Contents

The Cornhusker State

Nebraska is located in the midwestern United States. Its name means "flat water" in the language of the Oto Native Americans who once lived in the area. This was the name the Otos gave to the Platte River, which runs through Nebraska.

Much of Nebraska's land is covered in ranches and farms. In fact, 95 percent of the land is used for farming and ranching. This is more than any other state in the country. Nebraska's top crop is corn, which is why it is nicknamed the Cornhusker State. Farming communities in Nebraska once held **contests** to see who could take the dry, papery outer leaves, called husks, off the most ears of corn.

Rolling fields of corn like this one are a common sight in Nebraska. Nebraska produces more than 1 billion bushels of corn each year!

Plains and Rivers

Most of the land in Nebraska is part of the Great Plains. This is a wide area of treeless, grassy **prairie** between the Mississippi River and the Rocky Mountains. The land on the eastern edge of Nebraska is called the Dissected **Till** Plains. It was once covered in glaciers, which cut up, or dissected, the land. The movement of glaciers created the landscape's rolling hills and left behind rich soil. The Missouri River flows along Nebraska's eastern border. The Platte River runs across the middle of the state.

Nebraska has very hot summers and icy, cold winters. Nebraska sits in Tornado Alley, which is the name for a part of the country known to have many tornadoes.

Here you can see many farms in Nebraska along the Missouri River. The land you can see toward the top of the page, on the left side of the river, is South Dakota.

Making a Home on the Prairie

Until 1854, Nebraska was Indian Territory. Native American tribes including the Omahas, Otos, Pawnees, and Sioux **thrived** on the land, as they had for centuries. **Pioneers** passed through the plains on their way west on the Oregon Trail. They were not allowed to settle there, though. In 1854, the Kansas-Nebraska Act established the Nebraska Territory and allowed white settlers to move in.

The Homestead Act, in 1862, promised 160 acres (65 ha) of land to anyone who would come west to make their home. Thousands of people moved to Nebraska for the free land. More moved there when the Union Pacific Railroad set up its headquarters in Omaha. Nebraska became a state in 1867.

This picture shows settlers heading toward Chimney Rock, in Nebraska, around 1865. Settlers who were heading west used the rock to guide them.

Prairie Plants and Animals

Few trees grow naturally in Nebraska, but the state is home to the Nebraska National Forest. It is the country's only forest that was planted entirely by man. There are plenty of other plants growing naturally in Nebraska, though. Grasses, such as bluestem, grama, and buffalo grass cover much of the state's prairies. In the spring and summer, the prairie blooms with colorful violets, blue flags, columbines, and poppies. Nebraska's state flower is the goldenrod, which blooms bright yellow from July through October.

The bison that once lived on Nebraska's prairie are now mostly gone. Mule deer, badgers, coyotes, prairie dogs, and pronghorn antelope still make their homes in the state.

There were once millions of American bison on the Great Plains. Today in Nebraska, there are about 400 bison at the Niobrara Valley Preserve.

Giant Rocks to Show the Way

In central Nebraska, wind blowing across the prairie piled sand into hills. These hills are now mostly covered in prairie grass. This area is called Sand Hills. The Oregon Trail, which many settlers began following in 1843, brought pioneers through the Sand Hills on their way west. Along the way, the pioneers noticed unusual sandstone forms that rose up from the ground. The pioneers used these giant rocks as trail markers to show the way to other travelers.

The first markers the pioneers saw were called the Courthouse and Jail Rocks. The most famous of these markers is Chimney Rock, which rises 450 feet (137 m) into the sky.

Chimney Rock can be seen for miles (km) on Nebraska's plains. This is why it was such a good landmark for settlers. Today it is a beautiful and historic place to visit.

Turning a Desert into a Garden

The prairie land where Nebraska lies was once called the Great American Desert. Many people thought the land could never be good for farming. There were so few trees in Nebraska that the early pioneers had to build their homes from blocks of **sod**. Those hardworking pioneers turned Nebraska into one of the top farming and ranching states in the country! Nebraska's main crops are corn, soybeans, and meat. Nebraska farms also produce cows and hogs. The state is one of the biggest meatpacking centers in the world.

Nebraska is an important place for **finance**, **insurance**, and **real estate** businesses. **Transportation**, including railroad and trucking, is also big business in Nebraska.

A combine harvests corn on a Nebraska farm here. Nebraska is the third-largest producer of corn in the United States.

A Look at Lincoln

The capital of Nebraska is Lincoln. Lincoln is located in eastern Nebraska. It is the second-largest city in the state. The city was once called Lancaster and was founded in 1859. It became the state capital in 1867 and was renamed after President Abraham Lincoln.

There is a lot to see and do in Lincoln. You can visit the Children's Museum or the zoo. The Sunken Gardens is a beautiful place to walk. At Lincoln's University of Nebraska State Museum, you can find one of the largest mammal **fossil** collections in the United States. At the Great Plains Art Museum, you can see the work of painters who were inspired by Nebraska's wide open landscape. Lincoln is also the birthplace of the 9-1-1 **emergency** number!

Nebraska's state capitol is the third one to have been built in Lincoln. Finished in 1932, today's capitol has a 400-foot (122 m) tower.

It's Omaha!

Omaha is Nebraska's biggest city. It was named after the Omaha Indians, who once hunted buffalo on the land where the city now stands. The city was founded in 1854 and was Nebraska's first state capital.

Omaha is home to the Henry Doorly Zoo, the Omaha Children's Museum, and many other fun places. For those who are interested in history, there is a lot to see in Omaha. You can visit old meatpacking warehouses or take a walk around the President Gerald R. Ford Birthsite and Gardens. Visitors can also visit the Malcolm X House Site. Malcolm X was a **civil rights activist** who lived from 1925 to 1965.

Pumas and peccaries are neighbors in the Desert Dome of the Henry Doorly Zoo. More than 25 million people have visited this zoo over the past 40 years!

Visiting the Cornhusker State

When the pioneers first came to Nebraska, it was a wild land of grassy plains that seemed to go on forever under a big, blue sky. Thanks to the hard work of those pioneers, Nebraska now helps feed America with its many farms and ranches. It even has big cities like Omaha and Lincoln.

Being on the long, flat roads that go across the state can still give you a feeling of what it was like for those first brave settlers. At Homestead National Monument, you can see a log cabin and schoolhouse for early settlers. You can even follow the Oregon Trail through the Sand Hills and look for the Chimney Rock that once showed travelers the way west.

Glossary

activist (AK-tih-vist) A person who takes action for what he or she believes is right.

civil rights (SIH-vul RYTS) The rights that citizens have.

contests (KON-tests) Games in which two or more people try to win a prize.

emergency (ih-MUR-jin-see) An event that happens in which quick help is needed.

finance (fuh-NANTS) Having to do with money.

fossil (FAH-sul) The hardened remains of a dead animal or plant.

insurance (in-SHUR-ints) Protection against loss or harm.

pioneers (py-uh-NEERZ) Some of the first people to settle in a new area.

prairie (PRER-ee) A large area of flat land with grass but few or no trees.

real estate (REEL es-TAYT) The business of selling land and houses.

sod (SOD) The top part of soil that has grass growing from it.

thrived (THRYVD) Were successful.

till (TIL) Rocks of all sizes left by glaciers.

transportation (tranz-per-TAY-shun) A way of traveling from one place to another.

Nebraska State Symbols

State Tree
Cottonwood

State Animal
White-Tailed
Deer

State Flag

State Bird
Western
Meadowlark

State Flower
Goldenrod

State Seal

Famous People from Nebraska

Red Cloud
(1822–1909)
Born in North Platte, NE
Oglala Sioux Leader

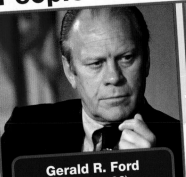

Gerald R. Ford
(1913–2006)
Born in Omaha, NE
U.S. President

Malcolm X
(1925–1965)
Born in Omaha, NE
Civil Rights Leader

Legend

- ◯ Major City
- ✪ Capital
- 〰 River

Lewis and Clark Lake

Niobrara River

Scotts Bluff
Chimney Rock

Lake C. W. McConaughy

Sand Hills

Fremont ◯

Omaha ◯
Bellevue ◯

Platte River

Grand Island ◯

Kearney ◯

✪ Lincoln

Missouri River

Republican River

Harlan County Lake

Nebraska State Facts

Population: About 1,711,263

Area: 77,358 square miles (200,356 sq km)

Motto: "Equality Before the Law"

Song: "Beautiful Nebraska," words by Jim Fras and Guy Gage Miller, music by Jim Fras

Index

Web Sites

Due to the changing nature of Internet links, PowerKids Press has developed an online list of Web sites related to the subject of this book. This site is updated regularly. Please use this link to access the list:

www.powerkidslinks.com/amst/ne/